WALK WAKEFIELD 1460:

A Visitor Guide to Battle-Related Sites

Helen Cox

**Herstory Writing & Interpretation/
York Publishing Services**

2011

Published by Helen Cox
Herstory Writing & Interpretation
www.helencox-herstorywriting.co.uk

Cover illustration: Sandal Castle, Wakefield, © Roger Keech, 2007

First published in 2011 by Herstory Writing & Interpretation/
York Publishing Services
ISBN 978-0-9565768-1-1

Also by Helen Cox:

Non-fiction:
The Battle of Wakefield Revisited, Herstory Writing & Interpretation/
York Publishing Services, 2010

Fiction (under the pen-name Rae Andrew):
The Lay of Angor: Gondarlan, e-book, Chipmunka Publishing, 2010,
www.chipmunkapublishing.co.uk; scheduled for paperback
publication 2011

Printed by: York Publishing Services, 64, Hallfield Road,
Layerthorpe, York YO31 7ZQ
Telephone: 01904 431213
Internet orders: www.YPD-books.com

CONTENTS

LIST OF ILLUSTRATIONS

PREFACE

Five hundred and fifty years ago, England was gripped by the long-running, vicious fight for the crown between the rival royal houses of Lancaster and York known today as the Wars of the Roses.

This little book will lead you through one of its most decisive encounters, the Battle of Wakefield, with an illustrated guide to visiting sites connected with the battle. With it, you can follow the whole of Richard, Duke of York's winter campaign of 1460 from the opening skirmish at Worksop to his fatal engagement at Wakefield, and on to the grisly aftermath at Pontefract Castle and Micklegate Bar in York.

Some places (Worksop Castle and Priory grounds, Sandal Castle grounds, Castle Grove Park, the Duke of York's monument, Wakefield Bridge and environs of St Mary's Chapel) are accessible to pedestrians at any time. Otherwise, all opening times and admission charges quoted at the end of each section are correct at the date of publication, but may be subject to future change; please check with the site concerned before your visit to avoid possible disappointment.

Helen Cox, December 2010

ACKNOWLEDGEMENTS

I am very grateful to Roger Keech for permission to reproduce his aerial photographs of Sandal Castle (cover and Plate VIII), and to Dr. Chris Tuckley of York Archaeological Trust for permission to reproduce the Trust's image of Micklegate Bar (Plate XVI).

I also thank David Cooke, author of *Battlefield Yorkshire*, for useful input to the Pontefract Castle section, and Kate Taylor, Chair of the Friends of the Chantry Chapel, for providing information about St Mary's Bridge Chapel.

INTRODUCTION: THE PRELUDE TO BATTLE

By 1460, three generations of Lancastrian monarchs had occupied the English throne. The first was Henry Bolingbroke, Duke of Lancaster, who usurped it in 1399 from his cousin Richard II, and ruled as Henry IV. He was succeeded by his son Henry V, the strong and popular king who won renown as the conqueror of France. But when Henry V died prematurely of dysentery in 1422, the crown passed to his infant son Henry VI – who grew into a mild-mannered, gullible man unable to live up to the promise of his great father.

Under his weak leadership, England suffered economic decline, defeat in the Hundred Years War with France, and corrupt government by royal officials leading to widespread discontent and civil unrest. In this turbulent climate, King Henry's cousin Richard, Duke of York, emerged as a champion of reform – and a rival contender for the throne...

Matters reached crisis point in 1460 when York, exasperated by the years of misrule, finally renounced his allegiance to Henry VI and (as a descendant of Edward III via both parents) resolved to press his own claim to the crown. His allies won a victory over the Lancastrian royalist forces at Northampton in July 1460, and took King Henry into 'protective custody'. The Duke then returned from exile in Ireland, marched to London and in early October, laid his hand on the throne in Westminster Hall.

York's peers did not immediately acclaim him as king - but his claim *was* strong enough for Parliament to pass the Act of Accord. This decreed that Henry VI would rule for the rest of his life, whereupon the throne would pass to the Duke or his heirs.

But Henry's wife, Queen Margaret of Anjou, refused to accept this disinheritance of their son Edward, the Lancastrian Prince of Wales. Fleeing to Scotland, she sought help to overturn the Act and restore the Prince's succession – ideally by wiping out the House of York on the battlefield. Many noblemen rallied to her cause including Henry

1

Percy, Earl of Northumberland, and John, Lord Clifford of Craven, who bitterly blamed York for the deaths of their fathers at the Battle of St Albans in 1455.

So as 1460 drew to an end, Lancastrian sympathisers from all over the country flocked to the port of Hull and the northern capital of York; and by December, an army of up to 15,000 was gathering at the great royal stronghold of Pontefract Castle. The Lancastrian lords did not wish to march on London, where the Duke had strong support and all the resources of the capital at his disposal. Instead they hatched a clever plan to draw the Yorkists north: despoiling the Yorkshire estates of the Duke and his staunch ally Richard Neville, Earl of Salisbury. The ploy worked – as the newly-appointed Lieutenant of England, York could neither ignore their rebellious actions nor, as a 'good lord', the plight of his tenants. He duly sent his eldest son Edward, Earl of March, to Shropshire to prevent the King's half-brothers, Jasper and Edmund Tudor, from joining the Queen's army. Salisbury's son Richard Neville, Earl of Warwick, would remain in London to safeguard King Henry; while York himself, accompanied by his second son Edmund, Earl of Rutland, and the Earl of Salisbury, set out for Yorkshire.

The Duke may have originally intended to make for Pontefract Castle, or the city of York, to set up a base for his northern operations. His army left London in early December 1460 and travelled up the Great North Road (the present A1), gathering supporters en route. At the same time, Queen Margaret's ally the Duke of Somerset was heading north-east from Corfe Castle with the Earl of Wiltshire, to join the rebel army.

On nearing Yorkshire, Richard of York discovered that his enemies already held Pontefract Castle in strength, and turned north-west off the main road to head for a convenient place to confront them: his castle at Sandal, near Wakefield. This quirk of fate put his army on a collision course with Somerset's advancing troops, and shortly before Christmas 1460, their paths intersected near Worksop – which is where our campaign trail begins.

Journeys to Wakefield in 1460

Figure 1: Journeys north in December 1460: York, Rutland and Salisbury headed NNW from London, following or parallel to the Great North Road; the Earl of March travelled NW to Shrewsbury, possibly via Brill and Towcester; Somerset and Wiltshire went NE to Pontefract via Bath, Cirencester, Evesham, Coventry and Worksop.

PART 1: THE 'BATTLE' OF WORKSOP

Worksop in north Nottinghamshire was a town with both Yorkist and Lancastrian connections. In the late 14th century its estates passed to Joan, the daughter and heiress of Thomas, Lord Furnival, then into the hands of the powerful Neville family when she married Sir Thomas Neville, High Treasurer of England. Sir Thomas was also a brother of Ralph, the first Earl of Westmorland – who by the marriage of his youngest daughter, Cecily Neville, became father-in-law to Richard of York. In 1406, the Worksop estates passed to the Earls of Shrewsbury via the marriage of Matilda, Sir Thomas Neville's daughter, to John Talbot, the first Earl. Talbot, a trusted captain during York's tenure as Lieutenant of France in the 1430's and 1440's, was killed at Chastillon in the final throes of the Hundred Years War. His son John, the second Earl, was initially on good terms with York, but by the late 1450's had become embroiled in the spiralling violence between the rival factions; he was involved in an assassination attempt on the Earl of Warwick in 1457, and killed three years later fighting for the Lancastrians at the Battle of Northampton. The title and Worksop estates then passed to his son, yet another John Talbot, who (understandably, given the circumstances) was York's bitter enemy.

Thus by December 1460 Worksop, an important market town and a crossing point of the River Ryton, was nominally held by the pro-Lancastrian third Earl of Shrewsbury. It was a stage on Somerset and Wiltshire's march to Pontefract, and also lay on York's path to friendly territory around Conisbrough, Barnsley and on to Sandal. Either or both armies could have headed there seeking recruits, supplies, or accommodation for an interim halt; but for whatever reason, they seem to have stumbled upon one another around 21st December. The 15th century *Annales Rerum Anglicarum* says that fore-runners of the Yorkist army (described as *praeeuntes*, which literally means 'goers-before') were 'cut off' by Somerset's men at or near Worksop. Unfortunately the original Latin manuscript is damaged at a crucial point – the number of Yorkists 'cut off' is missing! But it was probably small, since the *English Chronicle* says

4

that Somerset and Wiltshire were travelling with only 800 men, and no other historical or archaeological evidence has yet turned up to show that a major battle was fought in the neighbourhood.

So we don't know exactly what took place at Worksop. It may have been simply that a small group of Yorkist messengers or scouts ran into Somerset's contingent, and were literally cut off from the main army: either killed or captured to prevent them rejoining their oncoming companions or proceeding with their mission (possibly to warn Sandal Castle of the Duke's impending arrival). Nor do we know exactly *where* the incident occurred, although it may well have been in the vicinity of Worksop Castle. This was a motte-and-bailey fortification dating to the late 11th – early 12th century; it stood on the south bank of the River Ryton beside the road now called Bridge Street, whose name implies that the medieval river-crossing was located there, under the castle's control. Worksop Castle may already have been ruinous by 1460, given that its stonework had nearly all been removed by the time John Leland wrote his national *Itinerary* less than a century later. Nonetheless, it would still have provided a defensible position and possibly shelter for Somerset's troops if they had halted there en route to Pontefract; so perhaps this was where York's 'goers-before' rode into them as they all sought to cross the River Ryton.

But whatever happened, their encounter has left no trace around the modern town. So if you would like to start following in Yorkist footsteps at Worksop, all you will find of the castle is the low mound of its motte; even the river it dominated has changed course, though the line of the present Newcastle Street shows where it once flowed. However, the magnificent Priory Church of Our Lady and St. Cuthbert and its imposing gatehouse are well worth a visit. Dating to the 12th and 14th centuries respectively, these buildings would have been familiar to the opposing armies as they passed through the town. The Priory still houses the tomb effigies of their kinfolk Lady Joan and Sir Thomas Neville, and an interesting relic preserved in a tiny niche on the north wall: a fragment of skull pierced by a bodkin arrowhead. Unfortunately, this is unlikely to have any connection with the 'battle' - apparently it was found during building works several centuries before the Wars of the Roses - but there is the tantalising possibility that *somewhere* in the environs of the Priory or Castle, the real casualties of that obscure engagement might lay buried...

Information for Visitors to Worksop Priory:

Worksop Priory is open to the public on Mondays, Tuesdays and Saturdays from 9 am – noon, and daily for services. Further information about the Priory's history and special events can be found on the website www.worksoppriory.co.uk, by phoning Father N. Spicer at the Vicarage on 01909 472180, or by email to vicar@worksoppriory.tiscali.co.uk.

Further information on Worksop's history and Heritage Trail can be found on www.worksopheritagetrail.co.uk.

Directions to Worksop Priory:

Address: Worksop Priory Church of Our Lady and St Cuthbert, Priorswell Road, Worksop, Nottinghamshire

From the A1 South: Take the A57 towards Worksop/Sheffield. At the roundabout marked 'Lowtown/Clumber Park', turn right towards town on Netherton Road/Lowtown Road. Turn left onto the B6040 Cheapside, pass the Gatehouse and turn right onto Priorswell Road; you will see the Priory ahead.

From the M1: Take Junction 31 and the A57 bypass to Worksop. Turn left at the Netherton/Lowtown Road roundabout then follow the directions above.

To Worksop Castle from Worksop Priory: Take Memorial Avenue (off Priorswell Road, immediately opposite the Priory's west front) towards the town centre; you will shortly pass the Library, Museum and Tourist Information Office on the right. Continue straight on to Newcastle Street/Newcastle Avenue. The castle mound is on the left just past the junction with Bridge Street.

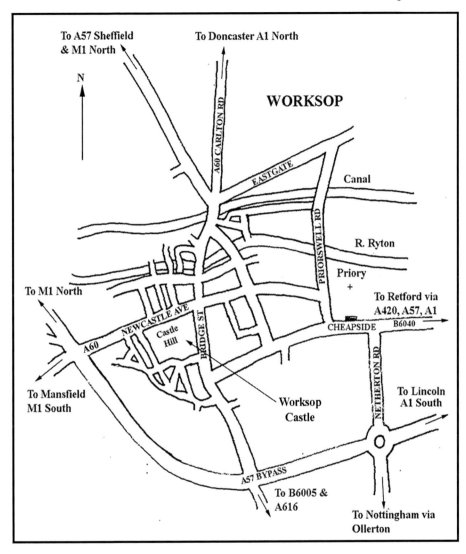

Figure 2: Map of Worksop showing the locations of the Priory, Gatehouse (marked by the black block on Cheapside) and Castle.

PART 2: THE BATTLE OF WAKEFIELD

Sandal Castle

After the skirmish at Worksop, the armies completed their respective journeys and by Christmas Eve at the latest, the Duke of York and his troops had arrived at Sandal Castle.

Like many English castles, Sandal was founded in the 11th century as an earthen mound and ramparts surmounted by a wooden palisade. It was built for William de Warenne, Earl of Surrey, who was granted the Manor of Wakefield by Henry I in 1106. In the 13th century, successive Earls of Surrey reconstructed the timber castle in stone to make a handsome, well-fortified lordly residence; then in 1347, the Manor of Wakefield and Sandal Castle passed to Edmund of Langley, first Duke of York, and his successors. In the mid-15th century, it was said to be one of Richard of York's favourite homes, adorned with painted glass and ornamental masonry depicting his heraldic emblem, the falcon. A number of improvements were carried out there during the brief reign of York's youngest son, Richard III, including the rebuilding of the keep's well tower (the New or North Tower); but after the death of this last Plantagenet monarch at Bosworth in 1485, Sandal Castle fell into disrepair. Its decay is documented in building surveys undertaken from 1538 - 66; then heavy bombardment in the 17th century English Civil War caused massive structural damage, after which it was further reduced by natural weathering and the activities of stone robbers.

Today, Sandal Castle survives only as the impressive earthworks of the motte and defensive ditches, the foundations and two standing wall fragments from the range of buildings in the Bailey, and the footings of the Gatehouse, Barbican and Keep. But in Richard of York's day it dominated the landscape south of Wakefield, enclosed by a 6m-high, 2-m thick curtain wall fortified by look-out towers, and with a massive stone keep towering from its motte. Sandal Castle was entered from the north, where some people believe there was once an outer bailey housing a smithy, barns, stables and the like.

8

There is certainly no space within the existing monument for such an 'industrial quarter', although since no outer bailey is mentioned in historical descriptions of the castle, the only way to prove or disprove this theory is through archaeology. So we can only guess that when York and his troops arrived shortly before Christmas 1460, they rode in through a cluster of workshops, stables and artisan's cottages, perhaps enclosed within a fence or wall; but the first building we definitely know they encountered is:

The Gatehouse

Dating to c.1250, this was a stout tower set in the curtain wall, with arrow-slot windows at ground level overlooking the approaches, and a crenellated battlement around the roof where sentries could patrol. It housed a small guardroom, and mechanisms to operate an iron portcullis and the drawbridge which spanned the huge dry ditch around the castle. Its defences had been improved c.1290 by the creation of an angled sloping passage, to make it difficult for would-be attackers to assail the portcullis with a battering ram.

Plate 1: The Gatehouse

As Plate 1 shows, the lower courses of the Gatehouse stonework, and the footings on which the drawbridge sat, can be seen beside the modern walkway over the ditch leading into:

The Bailey

Richard of York would have known this as a horseshoe-shaped courtyard less than 10m wide between, on the left, a crescent of imposing buildings consisting of his state apartments and substantial service quarters and, on the right, the ditch of the Barbican which guarded the entrance to the Keep.

Walking clockwise from the Gatehouse, the first structures you will see are the stone-lined Bailey well (originally at least 12m deep), and the foundations of the lodgings where Sir John Savile (York's Constable) and his family would have stayed. This is all that survives of a fine half-timbered building with ornate roof finials, but the remains of its toilet facilities are still visible: two garderobe shafts set in the outer wall, which would originally have been built up into a stone commode with polished wooden seats. Human waste simply fell down the shaft to discharge at the foot of the curtain wall into the ditch (which would have made it *very* smelly, especially in summer!).

Next to the Constable's Lodgings is the Privy (or Private) Chamber, shaped like a right-angled triangle to make it fit neatly within the arc of the curtain wall. The Privy Chamber was heated by a small hearth in its south wall, and had a garderobe shaft in the corner which it shared with the adjoining Great Chamber. A stretch of the curtain wall foundations can also be seen here, following the line of the ditch.

The Great Chamber survives only as the rectangular outline of its under-croft foundations. The under-croft was a ground-floor cellar originally used for storage; it had a stone flagged floor, a vaulted ceiling supported on a central pillar (marked by a square stone), and was heated by a fireplace in the south-west corner. Another garderobe shaft in its south-east corner served the upper floor, where living quarters for the Duke and his guests were situated.

Adjoining the Great Chamber was the Great Hall; here, part of the front wall with its large windows overlooking the courtyard is still standing. The Great Hall's under-croft was probably also used for storage; it had a stone flagged floor and two round pillars supporting a vaulted ceiling. The hall above would have functioned as the main dining area for the castle's residents, where (as food remains from excavations have shown) they feasted on a menu including venison, pork, beef, mutton, rabbit, domestic and wild fowl and fish.

Plate 2: The Great Hall

Next to the Great Hall you will see the gable wall and window of what was the most architecturally striking building in the Bailey range. Usually described as the Presence or Lodging Chamber, its first floor may originally have housed the castle's main chapel.

11

Plate 3: The Presence Chamber

Access to it (and also to the first floors of the Great Hall and Chamber) was via a stone staircase from the courtyard. The stairs led to a square porch and thence to a graceful semi-circular oriel gallery with numerous windows, both supported on handsome stone columns; the foot of the stair and column bases can still be seen in the external angle of the wall between the Great Hall and Presence Chamber. In the west corner, an area of cobbled flooring remains near the round stone footing of the pillar that supported the ceiling; and on the exterior wall, the rounded area of stonework on which a circular turret, capped by a decorative fleur-de-lys finial, once stood. At first floor level, this turret probably contained a spiral staircase to the walkway on top of the curtain wall.

The Presence Chamber completes the set of grand apartments where the Duke of York would have received, entertained and lodged his guests when they visited Sandal Castle on public occasions. Beyond it, the range continues around the southern arc of the Bailey with the footings of three buildings that formed the service quarters. The small Larder next to the Presence Chamber contained two hearths, and would have been used for the storage of bulk foodstuffs such as sides of beef and bacon, and barrels of salt and preserved fish. Adjoining it is a Kitchen some 10m square, originally provided with a roasting hearth, two smaller hearths and an internal drain that discharged into the Barbican ditch. As a 16th century drawing of the castle shows, the Kitchen had a pyramidal stone slate roof capped by a central timber louvre for venting out the smoke from its cooking fires (see Plates III and IV). Finally you will come to the Bake-house, substantially improved during the reign of Richard III; in the south corner, you can still see the base of a round oven where bread and pastries would have been cooked.

The Barbican

To turn now to Sandal Castle's defences: look over the inner ditch to the D-shaped footings of the Barbican, the formidable tower which controlled access to the Keep. Would-be attackers had to first cross a drawbridge over the ditch, pass through a gate protected by a portcullis, turn down a right-angled passage (to prevent the use of a battering-ram), and get through at least one more internal gate and portcullis before reaching a second drawbridge to the Drum Towers. The Barbican was designed to be held as a self-contained defensive unit; as well as housing the drawbridge and portcullis mechanisms it had a guardroom equipped with its own latrine, and a stair down to the sally-port in the ditch from which defenders could emerge to outflank attackers. Its walls were pierced with arrow-slits, and around the top were wooden targes (pivoting shields) between stone crenellations, giving protection and a wide field of fire to archers stationed within or on the rooftop walkway.

The Drum Towers

North-west of the Barbican you will see the fine masonry footings of two Drum Towers (Plate VI). These housed a drawbridge to replace the old timber bridge across the inner ditch; when this was drawn up, there was no way to access the Keep from the Bailey. Behind their gate and portcullis, a steep flight of stairs rose up the side of the motte between high stone walls. As well as giving dignity and grandeur to the approach, this stairway formed a last line of defence for the Duke of York's private residence – any assailants who succeeded in penetrating this far would be trapped in its narrow confines, exposed to missiles from defenders in the Drum Towers and Keep. To the right and left of the Drum Towers you will also see the only substantial remains of the castle's curtain wall, spanning the ditch and extending up the motte to connect the Keep in a solid defensive ring. The modern stairway follows the line of the north curtain wall to take you to the climax of your Sandal Castle tour:

The Keep

Plate 4: Barbican and Bailey viewed from the top of the Keep

The Keep gives magnificent views of the south fields once occupied by Sandal's deer-park, and beyond to the lakes of Pugney's Country Park; to the east, a superb perspective of the site; and to the north, the

14

battlefield area between the castle and Wakefield.

For Richard of York, this was a secure and luxurious home: a three-storey construction with four semi-circular towers, one facing west, the Well Tower to the north-west, and two facing south-east, built close together to form a gatehouse at the head of the approach stair. The towers had a basement level whose rooms (apart from the one containing the well) may have functioned as stores or prison cells; their upper storeys would have held private chambers equipped with garderobes and, (as suggested by finds of painted window glass with religious motifs), a chapel in the north-west tower. Although the precise internal layout of the Keep is unknown, the ground floor would typically hold a kitchen, store rooms, guard rooms and servants' quarters, with staff chambers and the main hall on the first floor, and on the second floor, the Duke's private accommodation.

These private rooms on top of the Keep could be where York and his seventeen-year-old son Edmund stayed in the run-up to battle, perhaps in the company of Richard Neville, Earl of Salisbury, and his sons Sir Thomas and John, Baron Montagu. Here the Yorkist lords could have enjoyed the brief respite of a Christmas truce to discuss their strategies, dine in the hall, and pray for victory in the chapel. From the Keep's windows they could have looked down on a scene bustling with war preparations: every building packed to the rafters with soldiers, supplies and armaments; carts laden with provisions and firewood trundling in; and beyond, a field of tents for the troops who could not be housed within the Bailey. The towers and wall-walks would have bristled with guards keeping watch for the enemy, and surveying the land where they expected to shortly do battle: the mile of ploughed fields and stretches of rough common, bounded by a loop of the River Calder, between Sandal Castle and Wakefield. And perhaps it was in the Keep hall where the Duke received an important guest on Christmas Eve: another relation by marriage, John, Lord Neville, who had come to request a commission of array to recruit on York's behalf. This promise of reinforcements was a lure the Duke could not refuse; but by granting Lord Neville's commission, he had unwittingly fallen into a fatal and well-prepared trap...

By Tuesday, 30th December, the large Lancastrian army including the Dukes of Somerset and Exeter, the Earls of Northumberland and Wiltshire, and John, Lord Clifford, had marched from Pontefract and taken up position on a ridge of high ground just south of Wakefield (see Figure 3). Many explanations have been put forward since the 15th century to explain York's decision to ride out and engage them. Some people believe he was simply stupid or negligent in not waiting for his eldest son Edward, Earl of March, to arrive from the Welsh Marches with reinforcements. Others suggest that he reacted rashly to Lancastrian provocation: the taunts of heralds, or an attack on one of his foraging parties to draw him misguidedly out to the rescue. Another school of thought says that the Lancastrians had concealed ambush parties in belts of woodland either side of Wakefield Green; and that when the Yorkists had deployed on the field, these hidden troops rushed out to surround and overwhelm them.

There is little or no hard evidence to support any of these theories – but there may be a more straightforward, militarily plausible reason behind the Duke's action. Certainly, the arrival of the Lancastrians had put him under great pressure; their army now lay between him and Wakefield, cutting off communications and supply lines and facing Sandal Castle with the threat of besiegement. But York deemed it unnecessary to wait for his comparatively small army to be reinforced by the Earl of March, because help had already come. Lord Neville had arrived with a substantial muster (the *English Chronicle* says he brought 8000 men, although this is probably a wild over-estimate); and according to one chronicler, Jean de Waurin, the veteran Calais commander Sir Andrew Trollope had also presented himself on the morning of the battle with several hundred more troops. So with the armies now much closer in size, the Duke saw no reason to delay and led his men forth in the confident expectation of victory. He may also have believed that when put to it, Lancastrian troops would defect to his banner; he was, after all, fighting (nominally, at least) for King Henry, with full parliamentary backing to suppress Queen Margaret's rebellion against the Act of Accord. If that was his belief, he was soon to find himself sadly mistaken.

Contemporary historical details of the action are exceedingly scarce, although if de Waurin's account is correct, the first shock for the Yorkists came when Trollope's troops launched a surprise attack (perhaps on a pre-arranged signal) on their supposed allies. If so, battle would have commenced with some panic and disorder in the Yorkist ranks although initially, according to the Tudor historian Polydore Vergil, the fight was 'mightily maintained mutually'. However, a much greater betrayal lay in store, because unlike many members of his family, Lord Neville had remained true to the Lancastrian cause. Unbeknown to the Duke, Neville had been one of the lords responsible for the harassment of his and Salisbury's northern estates; presumably, his request for a commission of array was the next stage in a clever plot to ensure York's downfall before the Earl of March could come to his aid. And so, when the Yorkists were irrevocably committed to action, Lord Neville led his contingent into the fray - not with the Duke, but against him.

With that, York's fate was sealed. Heavily outnumbered, his army was soon surrounded on every side – 'environed like a fish in a net or a deer in a buck-stall', as Edward Halle put it in the 16th century. His men tried desperately to flee; those who routed towards Wakefield were trapped in the bottle-neck loop of the Calder, and cut down in the area now known as Fall Ings. Among them was Edmund of Rutland, who was overtaken and killed before he could escape through the town. His father, attempting a fighting retreat, was overwhelmed by sheer weight of numbers and killed less than half a mile from Sandal Castle; and in the space of an hour, up to 2000 of York's followers were also lying dead on the field.

And even though the battlefield has now been largely obliterated by Victorian and later development, from the top of Keep it is still possible to see where the action occurred (see Figures 3 and 4 overleaf, also Plates VII and VIII) - then to complete your tour by visiting the sites where the Duke of York and Earl of Rutland died.

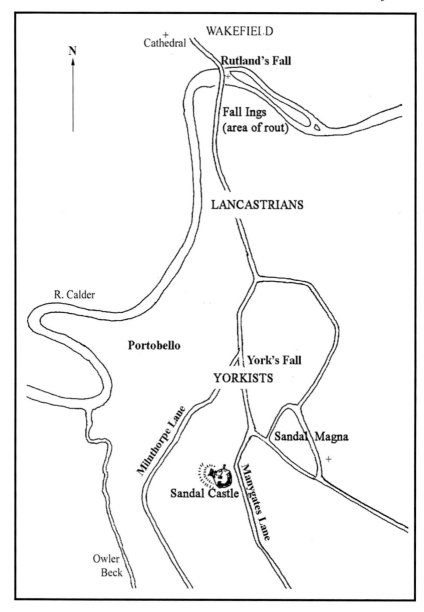

Figure 3: The Battle of Wakefield - 15ᵗʰ century landscape

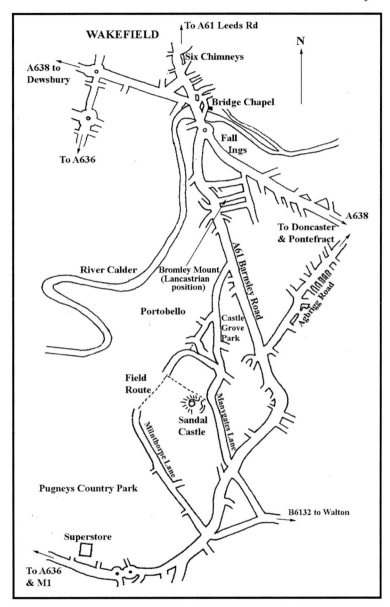

Figure 4: Modern Wakefield showing key battlefield sites

Information for Visitors to Sandal Castle:

Walkways around the monument give safe access for pedestrians, pushchairs and wheelchair users, but the steps up to the Keep are only suitable for ambulant visitors. There are interpretation boards at key points round the site, and a Visitor Centre containing displays on the castle's history, educational resources, a small shop selling books, gifts and refreshments, and visitor toilets.

Admission is free and the castle grounds are accessible to walkers year-round. The car-park gates are open from 9.30 am – 7.30 pm in summer, and 9.30 am – dusk in winter. The Visitor Centre is open from Wednesday to Sunday, 11 am – 3 pm.

Further information about the site and special events can be found on www.wakefieldcouncil.gov.uk/CultureAndLeisure/Castles/Sandal, by telephoning the Visitor Centre on 01924 249779, or by emailing to castles@wakefield.gov.uk

Directions to Sandal Castle:

Address: Sandal Castle, Manygates Lane, Sandal, Wakefield, West Yorkshire WF2 7DG

From outside Wakefield: Take Junction 39 off the M1 motorway (A636 Denby Dale). Turn left off the slip-road onto the A636 Denby Dale Road, signed for Wakefield. Turn right at the B6378 roundabout (Asdale Road, signed for Pugney's Country Park). Pass Pugneys on the left, continue past the large Asda supermarket and turn left at the double mini-roundabout onto Standbridge Lane (the A61 Barnsley Road). Continue to the traffic lights opposite the Three Houses public house and turn left, following the brown sign for Sandal Castle (Manygates Lane). The castle car-park is on the left c. 350m up Manygates Lane – beware the vicious speed-bumps!

From Wakefield City Centre: Sandal Castle is accessible by public transport (110 bus to Hall Green, alighting at the Three Houses); or by car (A61 Barnsley Road to the Three Houses and turn right at the traffic lights, following the brown sign).

Alternative Route for Walkers: Milnthorpe Lane/Old Pack-horse Road. Distance: c. 1 mile/1.6 km

Leave the A61 at Milnthorpe Lane (next to the Walnut Tree pub) and continue up the track (pedestrian access only) at the end of the metalled road. This approach gives an excellent view of Sandal Castle's southern aspect over what was once the stoutly-fenced deer-park where Yorkist soldiers may have camped and hunted in the run-up to battle. Where the path forks, bear right – this is the Old Pack-horse Road, a rough lane with an uphill gradient. Continue to the houses of the Portobello estate then turn right across the field, staying on the well-trodden path to avoid damaging the crop. Follow this path alongside the site's perimeter hedge to emerge on Manygates Lane, and turn right for the main gate and car-park.

Note: The ground is very uneven and may be boggy and slippery, especially after rain. Stout footwear is required, and this route is unsuitable for wheelchairs or people with walking difficulties. As it goes through private land and farmland, please adhere to the main paths, avoid dropping litter and keep dogs under control.

Plate 5: Approaching Sandal Castle from the south

Castle Grove Park/Duke of York's Monument
Distance from Sandal Castle: c. ⅓ mile/0.5 km

To continue your walk by visiting the best-preserved part of the battlefield and the site of York's fall, turn left from Sandal Castle car-park and follow Manygates Lane down the hill. This was the medieval road between the castle and Wakefield, and the route the Yorkist army would have taken to meet the foe on 30th December 1460.

On the right, past the mini-roundabout, you will see a remnant of Wakefield Green, now called Castle Grove Park (see Plate IX). There, on its well-preserved 'ridge-and-furrow' medieval field system, fierce hand-to-hand combat took place as the Duke strove unsuccessfully to fight his way back to Sandal Castle.

Opposite the park is Manygates Education Centre with York's memorial, a Victorian stone monument, set among its railings (see Plate X). Originally, the monument marked the site of his death slightly further to the north, near the junction between Manygates Lane and Milnthorpe Lane. In the 15th century this was a small hedged plot of land said to have contained a clump of willow trees by which the Duke made his last stand. A stone cross was placed there, perhaps by order of Edward IV, but unfortunately this was destroyed during the English Civil War. In the 19th century, the lost cross was replaced by this monument, which was subsequently moved to its present position when the site was developed.

Chantry Chapel of St Mary the Virgin
Distance from Monument: c. ¾ mile/1.2 km

Continuing down Manygates Lane towards Wakefield, try to imagine this urban environment as the open stretch of farmland where York's troops were surrounded and defeated. To your left is the modern Portobello estate, where human bones and fragments of weapons were unearthed during building works in 1825. Sadly, the fate of these relics is unknown, although a spearhead found there in 1959 is now on display in Wakefield Museum.

Where Manygates Lane joins the main road (the A61), turn left. The ground now begins to rise, and the top of this mild hill (Bromley Mount) is the most likely place for the Lancastrian army to have deployed prior to the battle. From the new bridge over the river, you can see the loop of the Calder enclosing the bottle-neck of land now known as Fall Ings, its name suggesting that many Yorkists were slaughtered here as they routed desperately towards Wakefield.

The site most commonly believed to be where Edmund of Rutland died is now visible ahead on the right: the medieval bridge and chantry chapel of St Mary's (see Plates 6, XI and XII). You can reach it by crossing the main road at the pelican crossing (there is also vehicle access if you are driving south out of Wakefield on the A61). The chapel was not, as some people believe, built to commemorate the battle; it dates to 1342 – 56, and is one of only three bridge chapels surviving in England (the others are at Rotherham and St Ives). It was originally a mass-house where priests would have prayed for souls in purgatory, but closed for this purpose in the mid-16th century and thereafter was used for various secular and commercial purposes. The fabric has been extensively restored since the 19th century and much of what you see today is Victorian.

Nonetheless, St Mary's may well mark the spot where Lord Clifford caught up with the fleeing Earl, and rather than ransom him to the Yorkists, executed him in revenge for his father's death at St Albans. (Another school of thought says that Rutland's flight may have taken him further north along Kirkgate into the city proper, where he was killed near a building called the Six Chimneys. This collapsed in 1941, but its location and name are preserved in the modern building erected on the same site – see Figure 4).

Information for Visitors to St Mary's:

Services (said Eucharist) are held at 4.30 pm on the first Sunday of every month, and the Chapel is usually opened on public holidays, during Wakefield Heritage week, and for special events. Visits outside these times can be arranged by contacting Kate Taylor, Chair of the Friends of the Chantry Chapel, on 01924 372748 or by e-mail to kate@airtime.co.uk.

Further information about St Mary's and its special events programme can be found on the Wakefield Cathedral website, www.wakefieldcathedral.org.uk, by telephoning the Cathedral office on 01924 373923, or by email to admin@wakefield-cathedral.org.uk.

Plate 6: East front of St Mary's Chapel

PART 3: PONTEFRACT CASTLE

By the late afternoon of Tuesday, 30th December 1460, the outskirts of Wakefield and the fields between the city and Sandal Castle were strewn with battle dead. The victors, whose losses were relatively slight, would have stripped the bodies of weapons and valuables, ransacked the castle and Yorkist encampment, and rounded up prisoners including the captured Earl of Salisbury.

And so, at the age of 49, Richard of York had lost both his bid for the throne and his life – but his story went on. The Lancastrians gathered up his corpse, along with those of his son and other prominent Yorkists, and marched off with them to Pontefract Castle – where you can pick up his posthumous fate…

The town of Pontefract had long been strategically important because it dominated the River Aire crossing on the Great North Road, the principal north-south highway since Roman times, and also guarded westward routes across the Pennines. This made it an essential place for the Normans to site a strong fortress, which in the late 11th century was awarded to Ilbert de Lacy as part of the large tract of South and West Yorkshire known as the Honour of Pontefract.

By the 15th century Pontefract Castle had become the administrative centre for the Duchy of Lancaster - and acquired a sinister reputation as a prison and place of execution for high-ranking nobles. James I of Scotland was held there, as was Charles, Duc d'Orleans, after the Battle of Agincourt in 1415; but perhaps its most famous victim is King Richard II. He was imprisoned at Pontefract by his usurping cousin Henry Bolingbroke (Henry IV), and died there in 1400 under suspicious circumstances – possibly from deliberate starvation.

As a royal stronghold, the castle continued to play an important role throughout the Wars of the Roses and beyond. Held for Charles I during the English Civil War, Pontefract was besieged several times and was the last Royalist stronghold to surrender – after which it was demolished at the request of local people, whose property and livelihood had suffered considerably from having such a dangerous prize in their midst. Although the barbican guard house survived demolition and was used for some years as a debtor's prison, the site's main 18th century function was as a place to grow and store liquorice, then in the late 19th century it became a public park.

But back in 1460, the castle would have been visible from miles away to the returning Lancastrian conquerors: a massive stone keep and inner bailey with six square towers in its curtain wall, looming from a sandstone promontory; its south-east facing gatehouse was protected by a substantial rectangular outer bailey, barbican and tower extending down the side of the hill. Somewhere within its precincts, perhaps in the inner bailey, the Earl of Salisbury, Captain Hanson, John Harrow, Walter Lymbrike and Sir Ralph Stanley were all beheaded on 31st December 1460 – as were the mangled bodies of the Duke of York, Earl of Rutland and several other Yorkist knights. The decapitated corpses were then interred in nearby religious houses, either St Richard's Friary or the Priory of St John (whose grassed-over foundations can be seen just beyond All Saints Church on the Knottingley Road) – but a more public fate lay in store for their heads...

Today, little remains of the ominous grandeur that was once Pontefract Castle. The outer bailey is gone, though as the street names suggest, its outline survives in the present South Baileygate (the A645), Castle Chain, Castle Garth and Micklegate (site of the barbican and tower). Like Sandal Castle, the present monument comprises an Inner Bailey, Keep and range of domestic and state buildings, although the standing remains are more extensive and substantial, as shown in Plates XIII – XV.

Visiting Pontefract Castle, the first structures you will encounter are the motte and drum towers of the large quatrefoil (four-lobed) Keep, where it is still possible to see some of the lower rooms and intra-mural stairs. As at Sandal Castle, the Keep's towers contained a well, store rooms, a chapel and lodgings, possibly including dungeons; perhaps this is where Richard II met his miserable death. From the Keep, walking clockwise around the site brings you next to the service quarters: Brew-house, Bake-house (with two large round ovens set in the wall), Great Kitchen, Scullery, Larder-house and Privy Kitchen.

Plate 7: The Kitchen range

Built into the curtain wall behind the service range are the square footings of three towers, the Piper, Gascoigne (Steward's) and Treasurer's Towers; then looking down the ditch behind the Larder-house, you will see the footings of the Swillington Tower. This was built at the start of the 15th century to improve defences on the north-western side of the curtain wall, and was originally linked to the castle by a wall-walk.

Beyond the Privy Kitchen is the range of state apartments, a Great Hall flanked by the Queen's Tower to the west and King's Tower to the east, where royal guests would have lodged. Perhaps a room in the King's Tower was where Richard III sent a letter to his mother, Cecily Neville, in 1484, '…written at Pontefract the third day of June with the hand of your most humble son, Richard rex'.

In front of the state range lies a free-standing Chapel founded in the 11th century and dedicated to St Clement; and beyond the King's Tower on the north-east side of the curtain wall, the remains of a second chapel constructed in the Elizabethan period. Adjoining it is the Constable's Tower, which, like the King's Tower, dates to the late 14th century, and was originally known as the Blanche Tower (possibly after Blanche of Lancaster, first wife of John of Gaunt).

Between the Constable's Tower and Keep are the remains of the Gatehouse, originally comprised of two flanking towers joined at the upper levels by rooms above the gate passage. The other visible features of the Inner Bailey are the revetment wall running from north-west to south-east in front of the Keep, and in the middle, access to a series of subterranean rock-cut cellars dating from the Norman period to the 15th century. These were used to store food and wine during the English Civil War, and as a prison for captured Parliamentarians during the third siege of Pontefract in 1648 - 9. The cellars are commonly referred to as 'the Magazine', although there is little evidence that they were ever used for the storage of gunpowder.

Information for Visitors to Pontefract Castle:

Entry to the site is via the main gate on Castle Chain, where there are two parking bays for disabled visitors. A walkway around the Bailey gives safe access past all the main features for pedestrians, pushchairs and wheelchair users, with seating and (rather battered!) information boards at key points. There are also steps up the Keep, only suitable for ambulant visitors. The Visitor Centre by the main gate contains a shop and displays on the castle's history; visitor toilets are in a separate block accessible during site open hours.

Pontefract Castle is open from Monday to Friday 8.30 am – 5 pm, and Saturday and Sunday 9.30 am – 6.15 pm (or dusk in winter). The Visitor Centre is open Wednesday to Sunday 11 am – 3 pm, and on Mondays and Tuesdays by request.

Admission to the site is free, but there is a charge (£2 for adults, £1 for children/concessions) to tour the Magazine (cellars). Magazine tours take place from Wednesday to Sunday, at 3.30 pm in summer and 3 pm in winter.

For further information about Pontefract Castle and special events, see www.wakefieldcouncil.gov.uk/CultureAndLeisure/Castles, call the Visitor Centre on 01977 723440 (or 01924 302707 for school visits), or email castles@wakefield.gov.uk.

Directions to Pontefract Castle:

Address: Pontefract Castle, Castle Chain, Pontefract, West Yorkshire WF8 1QH

By car from Sandal Castle: Turn left from Manygates Lane onto the A61 towards Wakefield. Turn right at the B6389 Agbrigg Road (just past the post office on the right). Turn right at the traffic lights onto the A638 Doncaster road. Where the road forks, bear left for the A645 to Pontefract. Remain on the A645 towards Knottingley and the Infirmary (Southgate), following the brown signs for Pontefract Castle. Look out for All Saints Church ahead on the left, and signs for the castle and car-park. Turn left at The Booths, up the cobbled hill; the car-park is on the left (4 hours free parking for visitors).

Plate 8: The landmark church of All Saints near Pontefract Castle

From the M62: Leave the M62 at Junction 39 and take the A639 south towards Pontefract. At the A645 junction, turn left towards Knottingley and the Infirmary (Southgate). Follow the brown signs for Pontefract Castle and turn left at All Saints Church/The Booths.

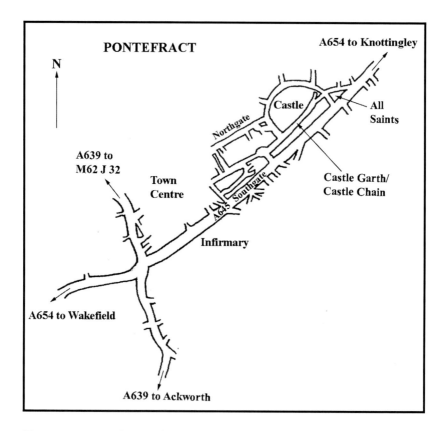

Figure 5: Map of Pontefract

PART 4: MICKLEGATE BAR & YORK WALLS

Events at Pontefract Castle on 31st December 1460 set the stage for the last act of the Battle of Wakefield: a gruesome aftermath destined to have fateful consequences for the Lancastrian victors.

The beheading of prominent Yorkist captives and corpses was deeply significant to medieval minds: a deliberate dishonouring fuelled by hatred and vengeance whose effects continued into the afterlife, since the separation of body and head would deny the victims' physical resurrection when the Day of Judgement came. Afterwards, the Lancastrians mounted the heads (the Duke's distinguished by a mocking paper crown) on stakes 'for a spectacle to the people and a terror to the rest of the adversaries', and carried them to the walled city of York.

York, situated at the confluence of the Rivers Ouse and Foss, had been one of the principal cities in England for more than a thousand years. The Romans named it Eboracum and protected it with strong stone walls; to the Vikings, who captured it in AD 866, it became the major trading settlement of Jorvik; and its importance was recognised by William the Conqueror, who built two castles there, York Castle and Baile Hill, to control it. Baile Hill survives only as part of the motte and rampart built into the city walls; but Clifford's Tower, constructed by Henry III between 1245 – 65 to replace the old timber tower of York Castle, is still standing.

By the 15th century, York had become the second largest city after London and effectively the capital of northern England. Micklegate Bar, built and developed between the 12th – 14th centuries, was the most important of its four gates; the main north-south highway passed through it, and it acted as the focus for civic events including welcoming visiting sovereigns to York (Henry VI had been received there with great ceremony in 1448).

So delivering the Duke of York's head to Micklegate Bar and displaying it there on a spike was a calculated act: a reminder to the populace of the consequences of rebellion against their anointed king, and an example of Lancastrian black humour so that, as Queen Margaret is made to quip in Shakespeare's *King Henry VI, Part 3*, 'York may overlook the town of York'. The heads of the Earls of Rutland and Salisbury were mounted alongside, while those of Sir Ralph Stanley and the rest of the victims were displayed on the other gates for people approaching York from any direction to be confronted by the horror.

Information for Visitors to Micklegate Bar:

Micklegate Bar re-opened to the public in May 2010 with new displays on its history on the first and second floors. Entry is from the city wall, and admission to the shop at this level is free. Admission to the upper display floors costs £3.50 for adults, £2.50 for concessions, and is free for children accompanied by a paying adult or to York residents on proof of residency; the ticket gives 12 months free admission from the date of purchase. The stairs to the display floors are quite steep, and there are no toilets or wheelchair access.

The building is open 7 days a week from 10 am - 3pm (last admission) between 1st February and 31st October, and from 11 am - 3 pm throughout November. Micklegate Bar is closed for the winter from 1st December to 31st January.

For further information about the site and special events, see www.micklegatebar.com, email micklegatebar@yorkat.co.uk or phone 01904 634191 for bookings.

Directions to Micklegate Bar:

Micklegate Bar is situated on Micklegate, just off the A1036 Inner Ring Road by the junction with Blossom Street (leading to the A64 Leeds and A1). There is no parking at the site, but it is within easy walking distance of York Railway Station, which has a long-stay car-park behind it serving the National Railway Museum.

York City Walls

Micklegate Bar is only one point of interest on York's city walls. If you would like to continue your tour, you can walk a 2.5 mile/4 km circuit around these impressive defences, where 34 of the original 39 towers and the other three historic gates remain intact. Bootham Bar to the west of York Minster stands on the site of one of the gateways into the Roman fortress built by the IX Legion in AD 71; the earliest stonework surviving today is Norman, but most of the structure dates to the 14th century. Walmgate Bar, at the junction with the A1079 to Hull, is the only gate where the barbican has survived. Monk Bar, east of the Minster, dates to the 14th century with a top floor added in the late 15th century; it is the most elaborate of the four gates and houses the Richard III Museum.

Information for Visitors to York City Walls:

Admission to the City Walls is free, and they are open every day of the year except Christmas Day from 8 am to dusk, unless rendered too dangerous by ice or bad weather conditions. The walkways are relatively narrow, with steep steps and sheer unguarded drops which make them unsuitable for visitors who suffer from vertigo or fear of heights. For Health & Safety reasons, children must be carefully supervised, cycling is forbidden, there is no wheelchair access and no dogs other than guide dogs are permitted.

For further information, see the City Walls section on the Micklegate Bar website www.micklegatebar.com. This provides details of the full circuit and all sites of interest around it from the Roman period to the present day, including route guides, activity sheets and a downloadable map. Under 'Vodcast' you will also find three short video guides covering the northern section from Bootham Bar to Monk Bar, which can be viewed on your PC or downloaded to an iPod or mobile phone.

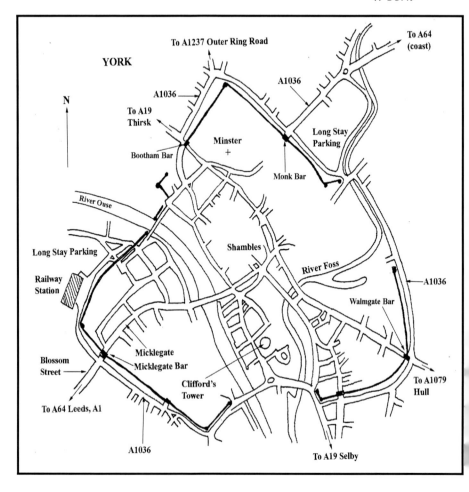

Figure 6: Map of York showing city walls (bold black line), Micklegate Bar and the other historic gateways

POSTSCRIPT

So ended the Battle of Wakefield and the last journey of Richard of York – but his cause did not die with him. News of his death and dishonour reached Shrewsbury in January 1461, whereupon the Earl of March embarked upon a bloody campaign of vengeance which culminated at Towton on Palm Sunday, March 29th. Queen Margaret's victory had been short-lived; her great army was destroyed, she and Henry VI driven into exile, and her hated enemy's eldest son assumed the crown as King Edward IV. One of the new king's first acts was to reunite the heads and bodies of his father and younger brother in Pontefract; then in July 1476, he had them exhumed and reburied with suitable pomp at Fotheringhay Castle... but that's another story!

RELATED PLACES OF INTEREST

Wakefield Museum, Wood Street, Wakefield WF1 2EW:
Archaeology displays including Sandal Castle in the Wars of the Roses and English Civil War. Free admission, open Tuesday to Saturday 10.30 am – 4 pm. Telephone 01924 305356, or see www.wakefield.gov.uk/CultureAndLeisure/Museums/Wakefield

Wakefield Cathedral, Northgate, Wakefield WF1 IHG:
Magnificent Norman and medieval architecture containing some fine 15th century carved woodwork. Open daily for public visits and services. Telephone 01924 373923, email admin@wakefield-cathedral.org.uk, or see www.wakefieldcathedral.org.uk.

Pontefract Museum, Salter Row, Pontefract WF8 1BA:
Displays include the history of Pontefract Castle and Civil War sieges. Free admission, open Monday to Friday 10 am – 4.30 pm, Saturday 10.30 am – 4.30 pm. Telephone 01977 722740, or see www.wakefield.gov.uk/CultureAndLeisure/Museums/Pontefract

FURTHER RESOURCES

Butler, L., *Sandal Castle, Wakefield: The History and Archaeology of a Medieval Castle*, Wakefield Historical Publications, 1991.

Cox, H., *The Battle of Wakefield Revisited: a fresh perspective on Richard of York's final battle, December 1460*, Herstory Writing & Interpretation/York Publishing Services, 2010.

Haigh, P.A., *The Battle of Wakefield 1460*, Sutton Publishing Ltd., 1996.

Mayes, P., & Butler, L., *Sandal Castle Excavations 1964 – 1973*, Wakefield Historical Publications, 1983.

Roberts, I., et al, *Pontefract Castle Archaeological Excavations 1982 – 86*, Yorkshire Archaeology Vol. 8, West Yorkshire Archaeology Service, 2002.

An excellent digital reconstruction of Sandal Castle and discussion of the battle can be found on the DVD *Sandal Castle: The Battle of Wakefield 1460 & Building Sandal's Castles* by John L. Fox, www.loyaltybindsme.com.

Plates I and II: Worksop Priory and Gatehouse

Plates III and IV: As it was – reconstruction model of 15th century Sandal Castle in the Visitor Centre, and as seen in a 16th century perspective drawing

Plate V: Sandal Castle today - the standing remains
Plate VI: Barbican, Drum Towers and Sally-port

River Calder

Rutland's Fall

Fall Ings

Portobello

York's Fall

Castle Grove Park

Area of Yorkist camp

Manygates Lane

Area of deer-park

Plates VII and VIII: The battlefield from the top of the Keep and from the air (aerial photograph ©Roger Keech 2007)

Plates IX and X: Castle Grove Park and York's monument

Plates XI and XII: St Mary's chapel, exterior and interior

Plates XIII and XIV: Pontefract Castle, Drum Towers and Keep

Plates XV and XVI: Pontefract Inner Bailey and Micklegate Bar
(Bar photograph © York Archaeological Trust)